Picture Puzzle

Match the Elephant Parts

Add ears, eyes, trunk, legs, and tail stickers to complete the elephant's body.

T0039847

sticker sticker sticker sticker

sticker

sticker sticker sticker

Picture Puzzle

Match the Zebra Parts

Add ear, eye, nose, legs, and tail stickers to complete the zebra's body.

sticker

sticker

sticker

sticker

sticker

sticker

Creativity

Make a Pattern on the Giraffe

Add stickers to the giraffe to create its pattern.

Creativity

In the Sea

Put stickers wherever you'd like to create an underwater scene.

Creativity

In the Sky

Put stickers wherever you'd like to create a scene in the sky.

Picture Puzzle

On a Safari

What animals do you see on a safari? Put each animal sticker on its matching shadow.

sticker

sticker

sticker

sticker

sticker

Picture Puzzle

On a Farm

What animals do you see on a farm? Put each animal sticker on its matching shadow. Then, give each animal a sticker of what they would like.

Matching Game

Guess the Animal

Guess the animal from its body part. When you identify the animal, put a sticker on its shadow.

sticker

sticker

sticker

sticker

Matching Game

Vehicle Match

Each picture shows the front of a vehicle. Put a sticker next to the vehicle that shows it from the side.

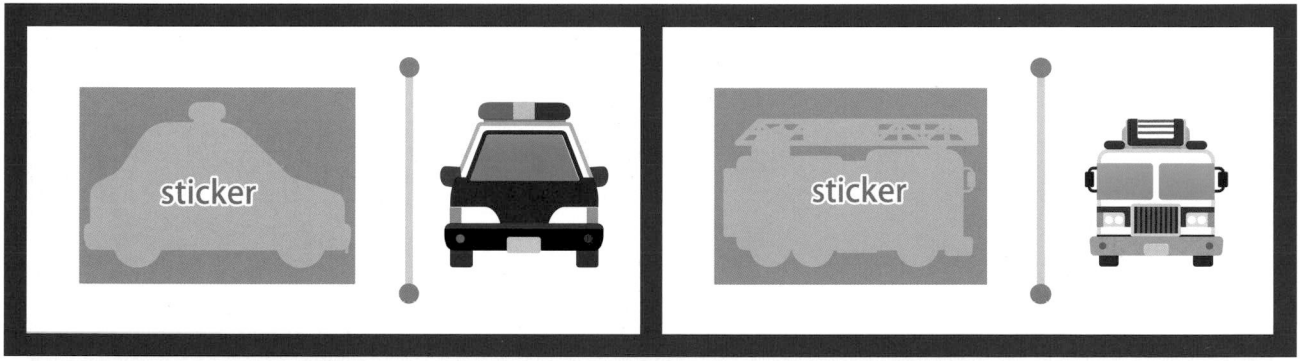

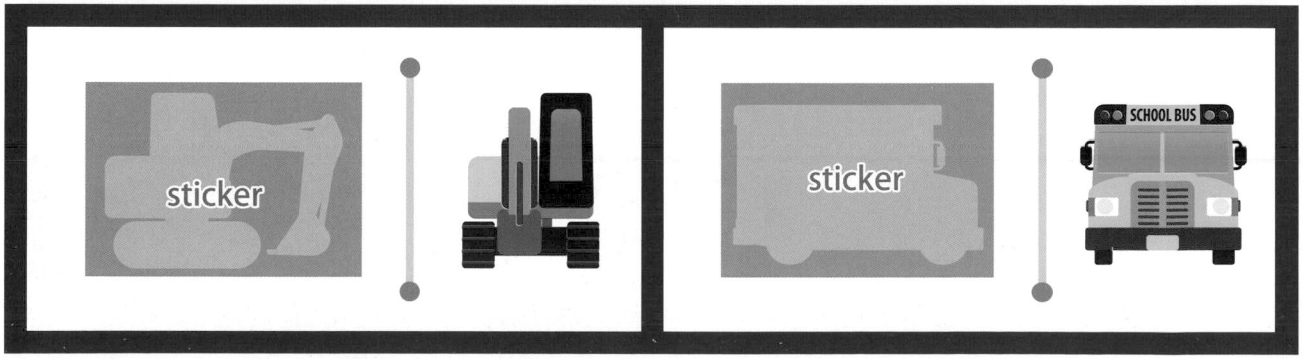

Classification

These Things Go Together

Find the stickers that go together and put them in each group (for example: vehicles, animals, fruit).

vehicles

sticker

sticker

sticker

animals

sticker

sticker

sticker

fruit

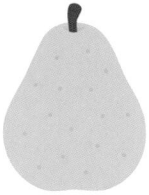

sticker

sticker

sticker

Picture Puzzle

Complete the Picture

Put the matching sticker next to each object to complete the picture.

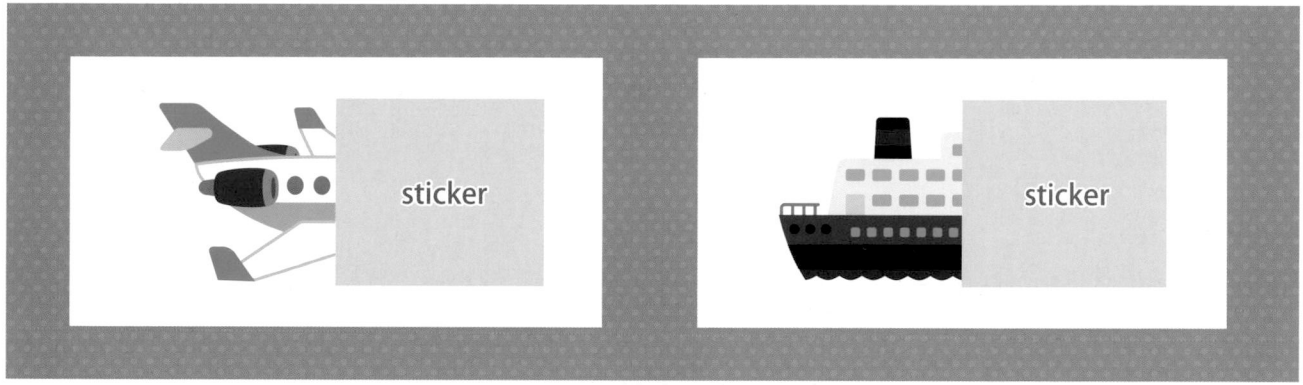

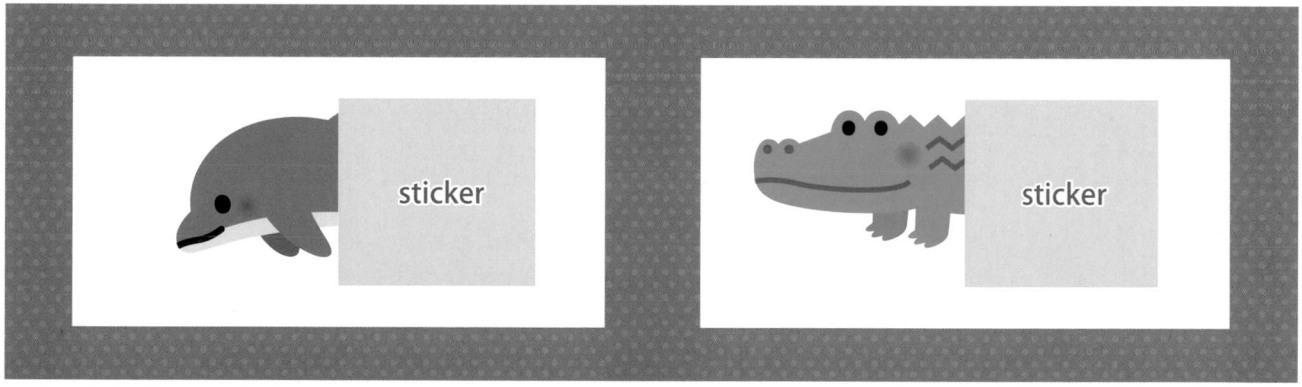

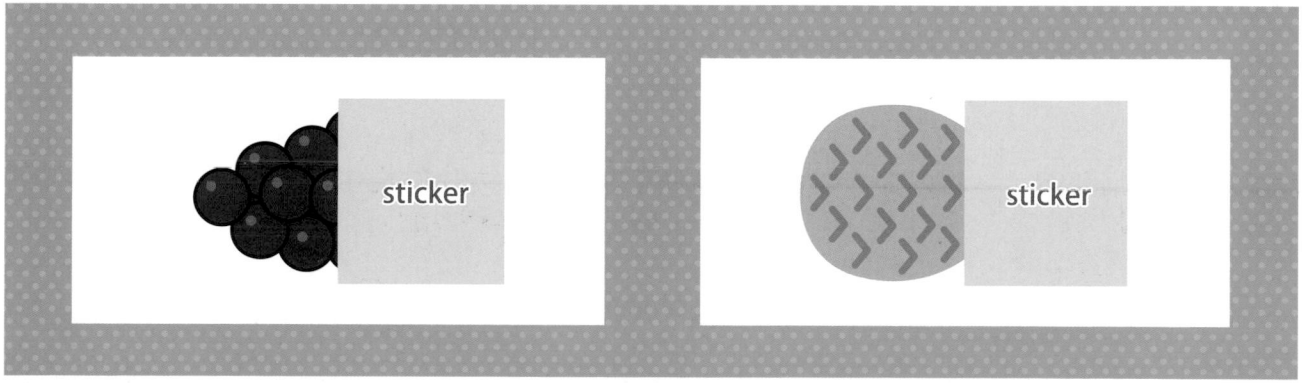

Picture Puzzle

Finish the Picture

Add stickers to finish each picture so that it matches the example.

example

example

Picture Puzzle

Picture Scramble

Do you know the animal in the scrambled picture? Name the animal, then add stickers to complete the picture.

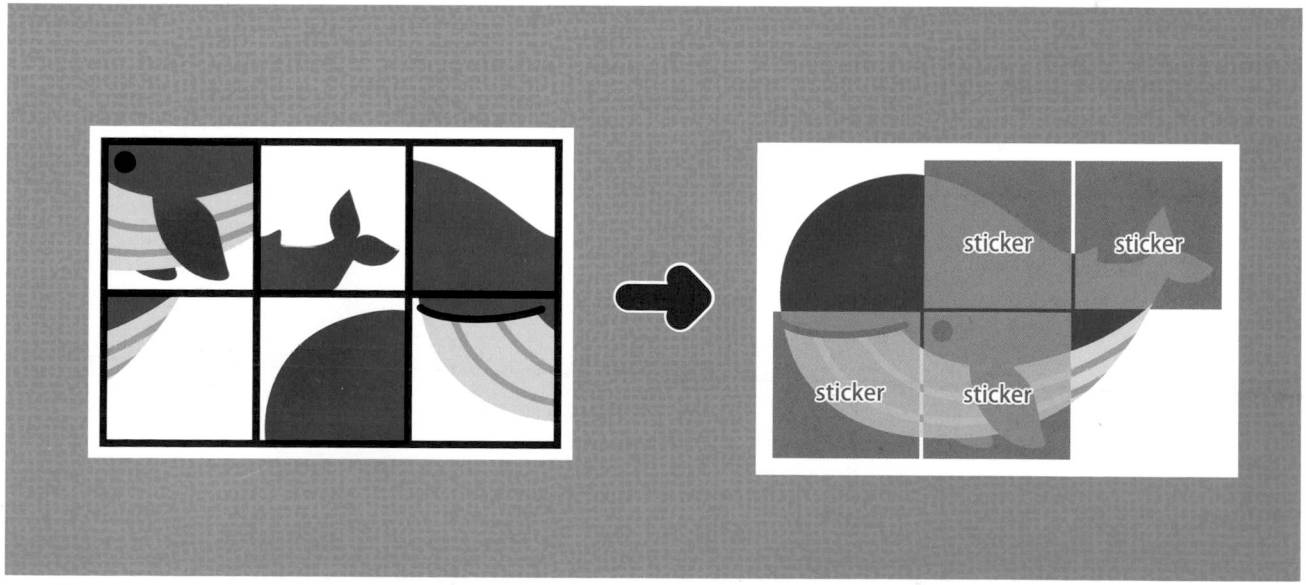

Matching Game

Animal Search

Find the animals hidden in the picture. Then, put the matching sticker in the box.

sticker

sticker

sticker

sticker

Matching Game

Vegetable Search

Find the vegetables hidden in the picture. Then, put the matching sticker in the box.

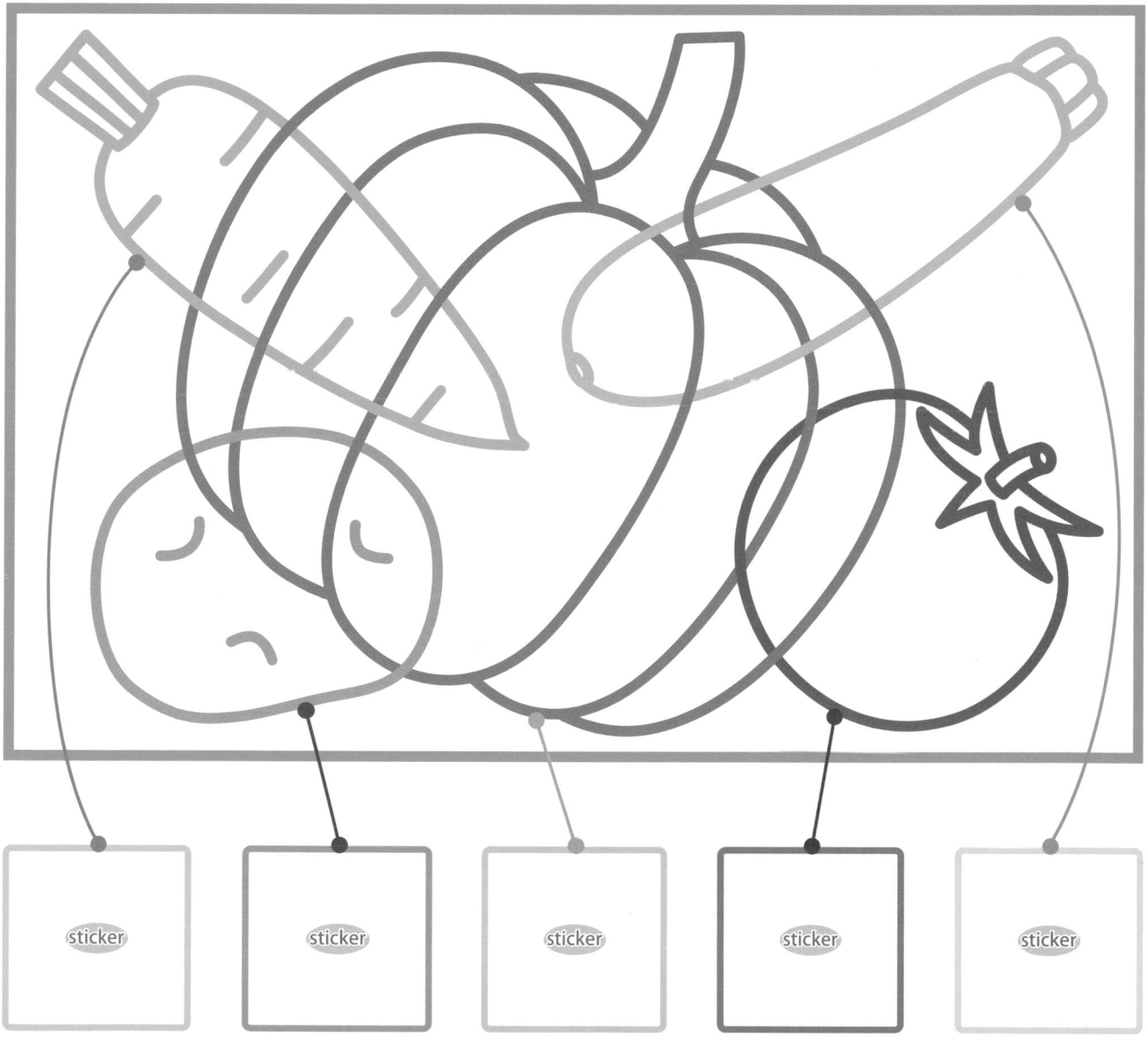

Numbers

Busy Garden

Put a bee sticker on each flower.

Numbers

Hungry Hamsters

Give each hamster a seed sticker.

Numbers

Make a Stylish Ghost

Put a bow tie sticker on each ghost.

Creativity

Make a Funny Monster

Put eyes, nose, mouth, and arms stickers on each monster.

Pattern Puzzle

Follow the pattern in the example to create the same pattern in the boxes on the right.

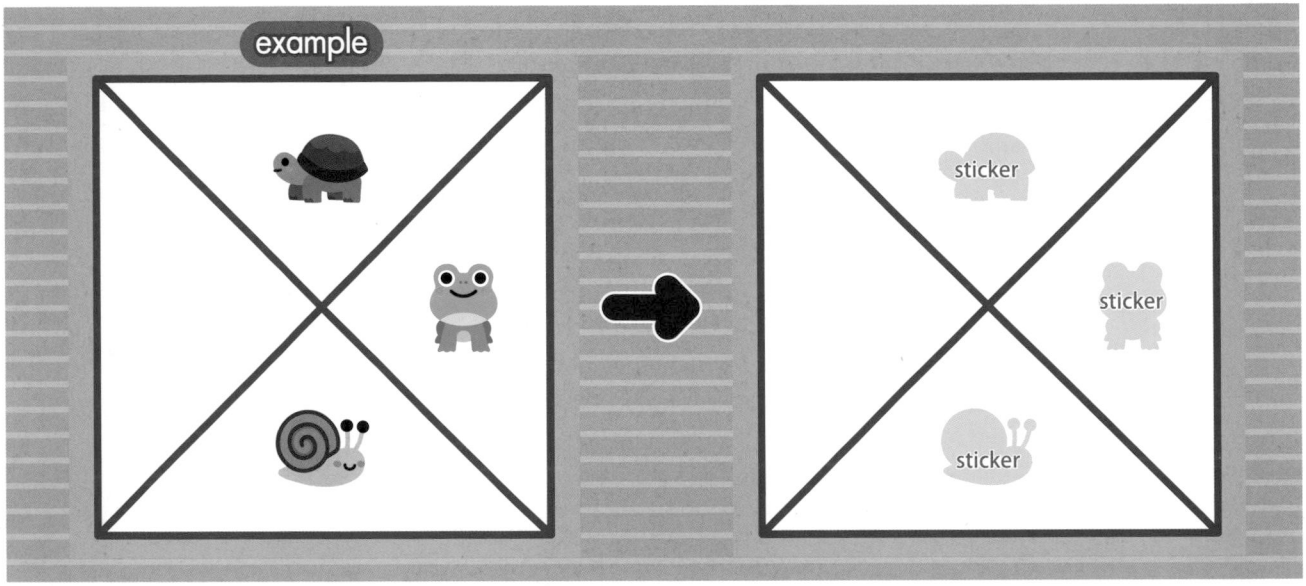

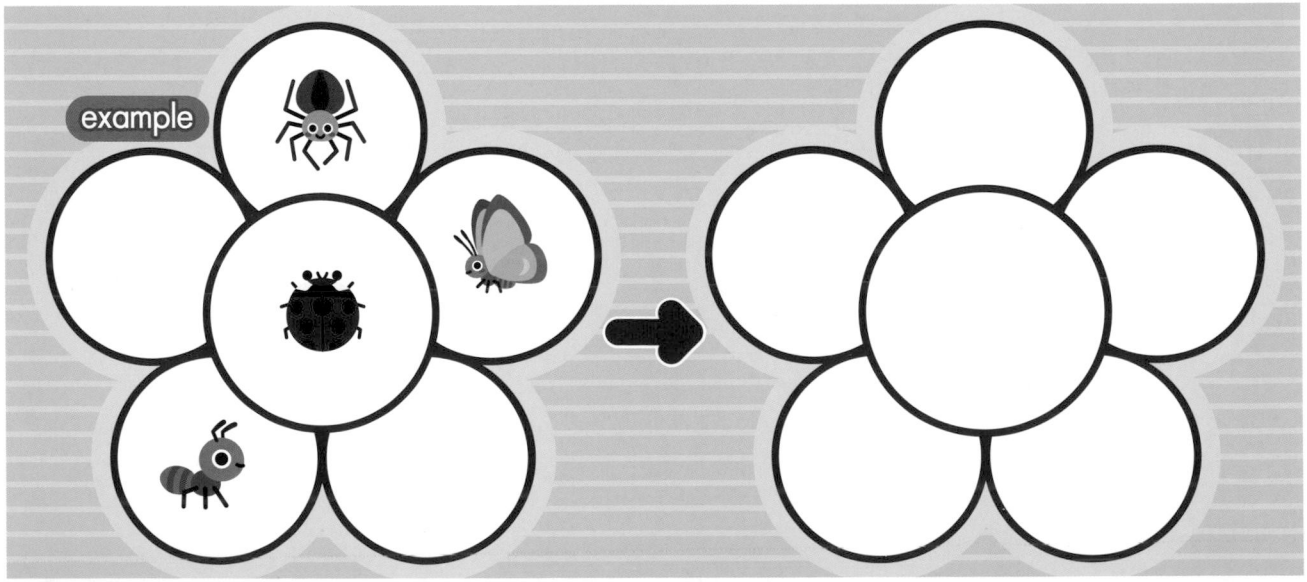

Pattern Puzzle

Follow the pattern in the example to create the same pattern in the boxes on the right.

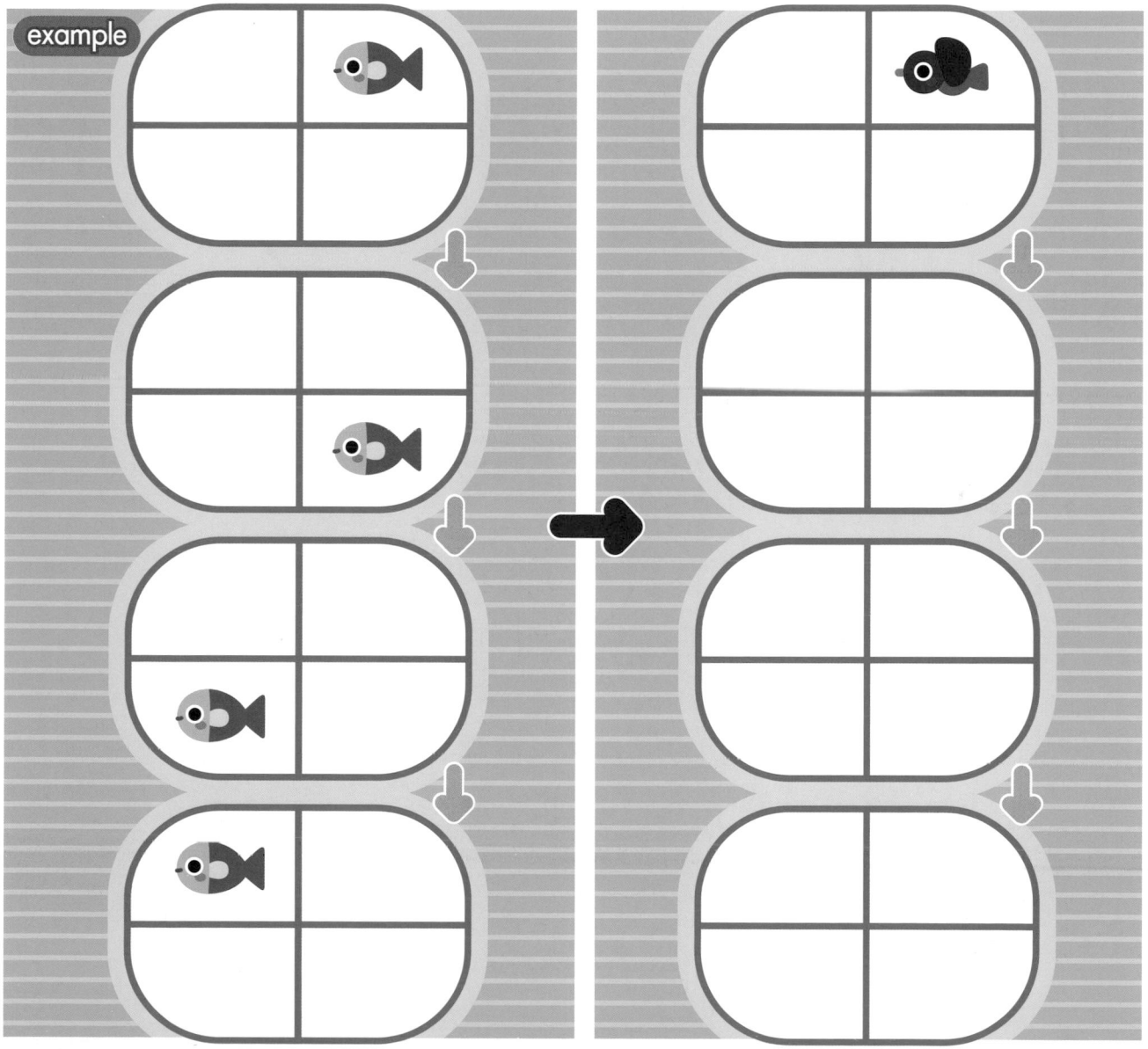

Picture Puzzle

What Is Missing?

Add fruit stickers to the bottom plate so it matches the top plate.

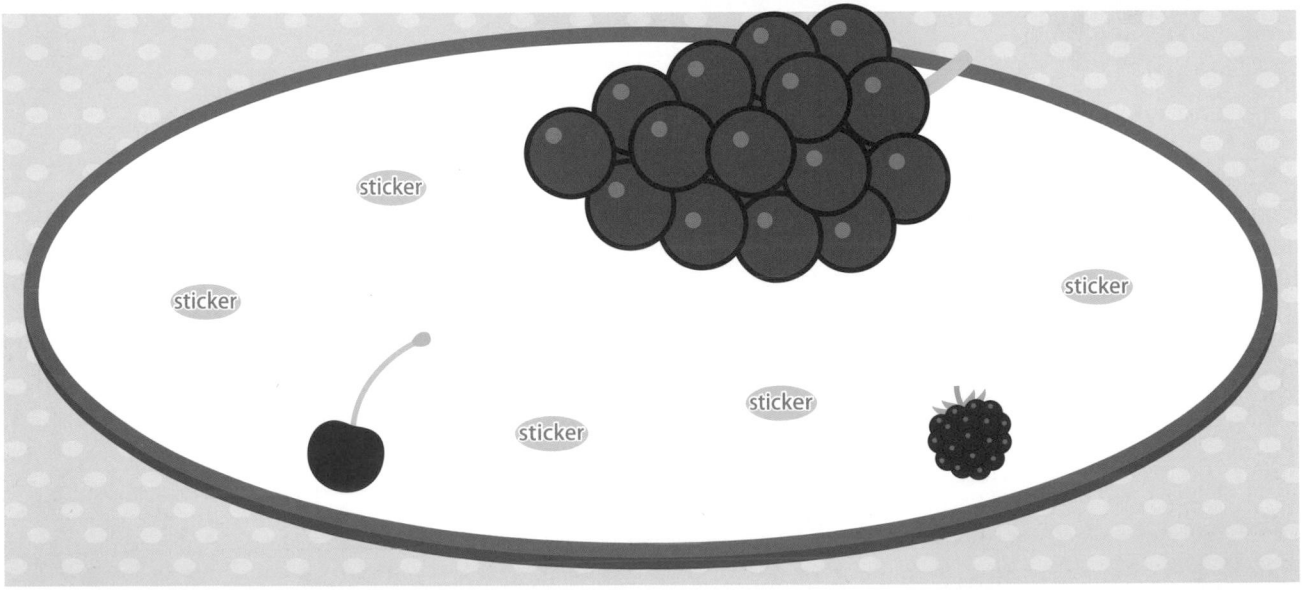

Matching Game

Match the Shadows

The shadows on the left are made up of three fruits. Find the missing fruit stickers and add them to each group.

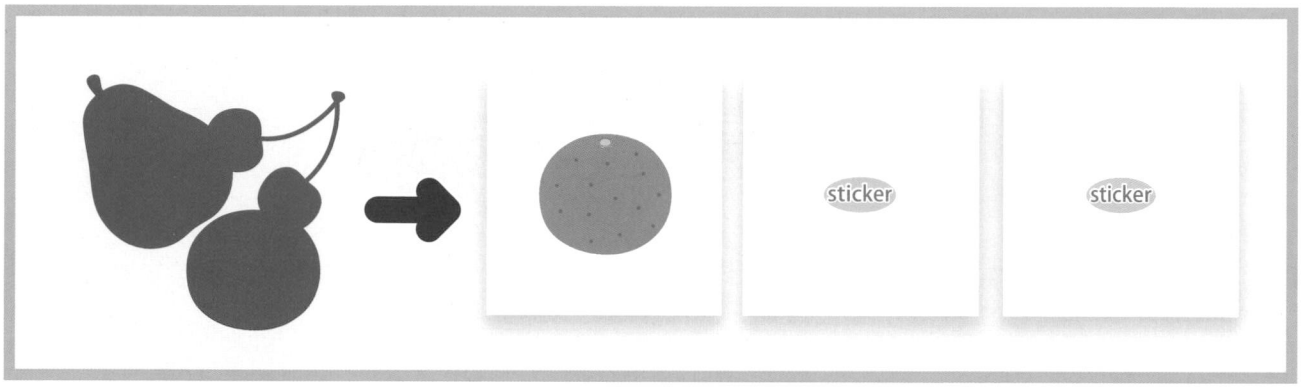

Picture Puzzle

Length and Height

Put each snake sticker in the blank space that matches its size.
Then, do the same for the giraffe stickers.

Picture Puzzle

Weight and Size

Match the animal stickers to their shadows, then put extra stickers anywhere you'd like. Which animal is heavier? Which animal is bigger?

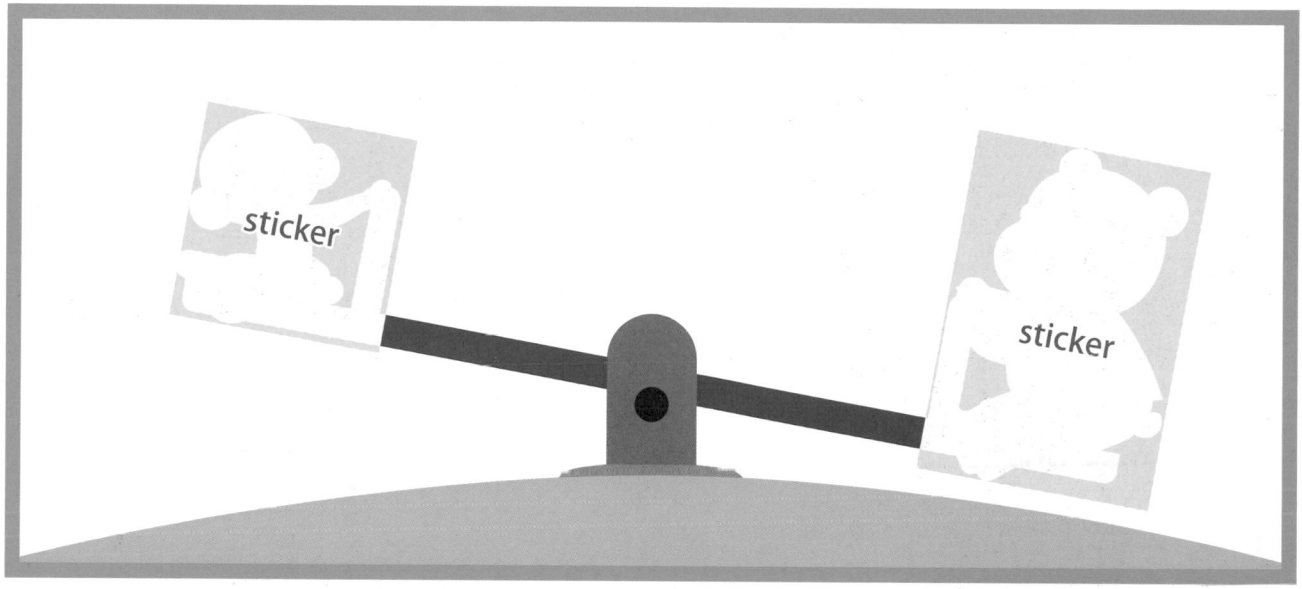

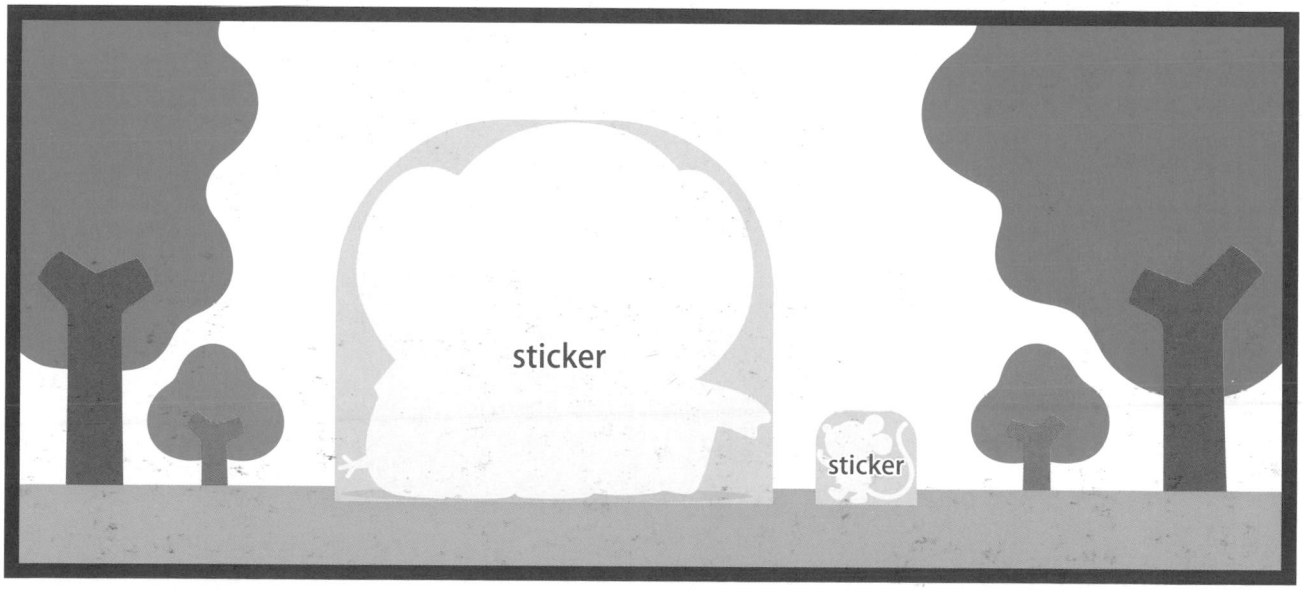

Letters

Things That Start with A

Say the name of each thing in the letter A. Then, put the matching sticker on sticker.

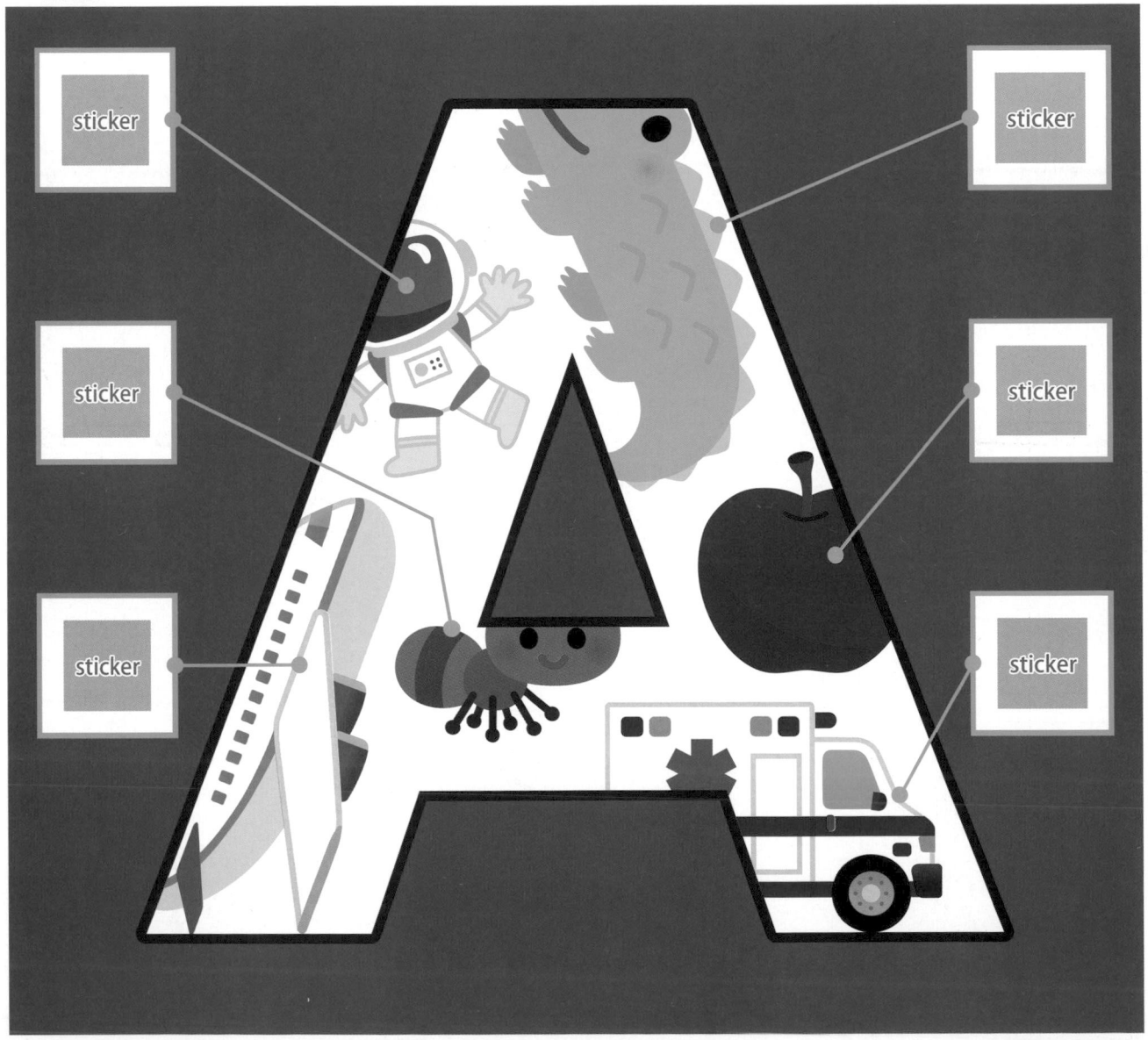

Letters

Things That Start with B

Say the name of each thing in the letter B. Then, put the matching sticker on sticker.

Letters

ABC Maze

Sticker

Good job!

Follow the path in the order of the alphabet. As you go, put the letter stickers on the path. Then, put stickers on the matching sticker.

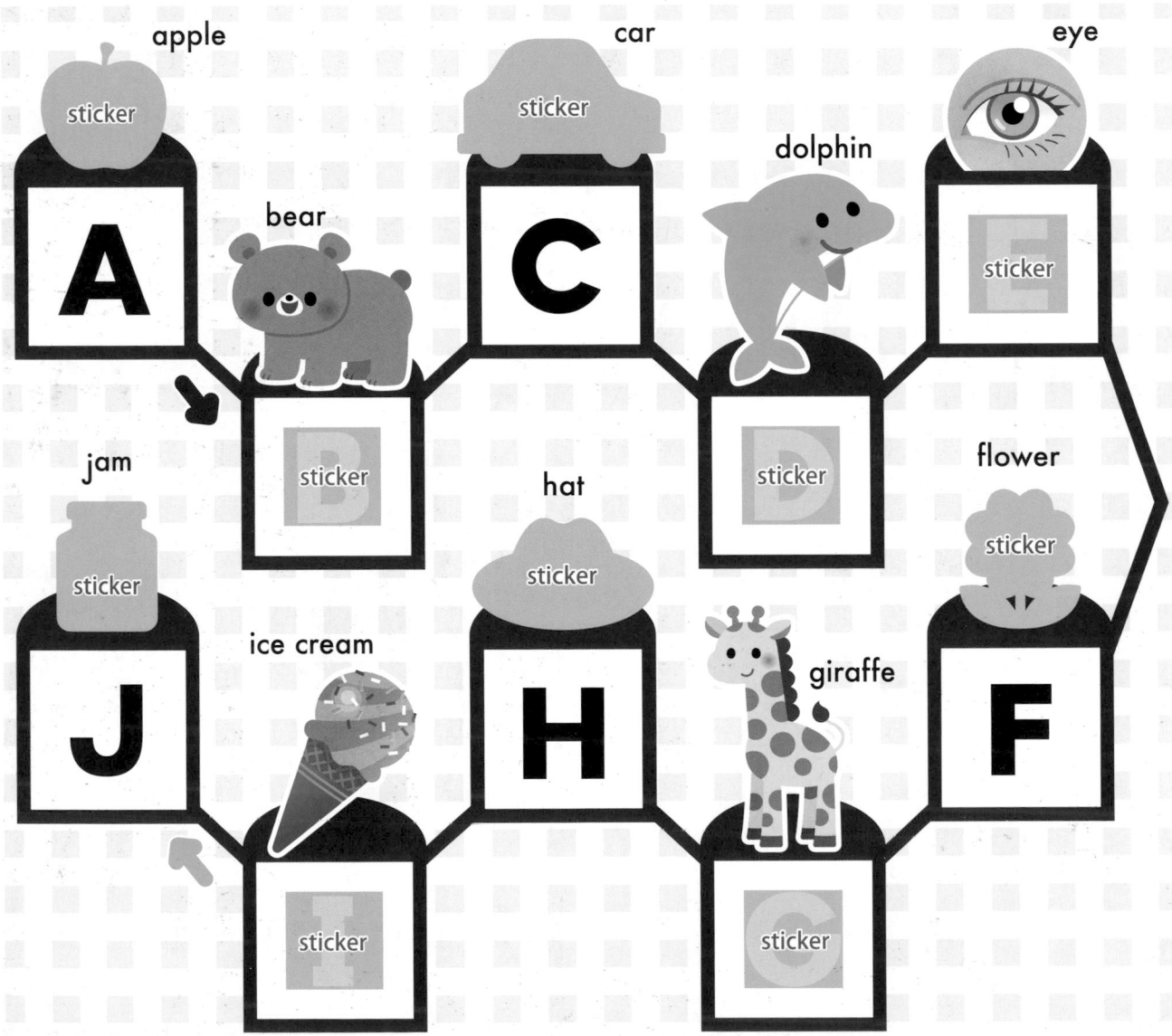

Numbers and Quantity

Add stickers on sticker so the number of frogs matches the number in the box.

Numbers and Quantity

Add stickers on sticker so the number of stars matches the number in the box.

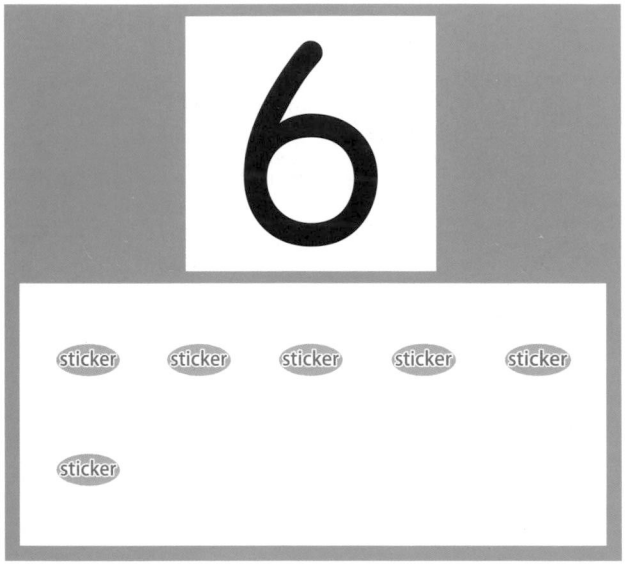

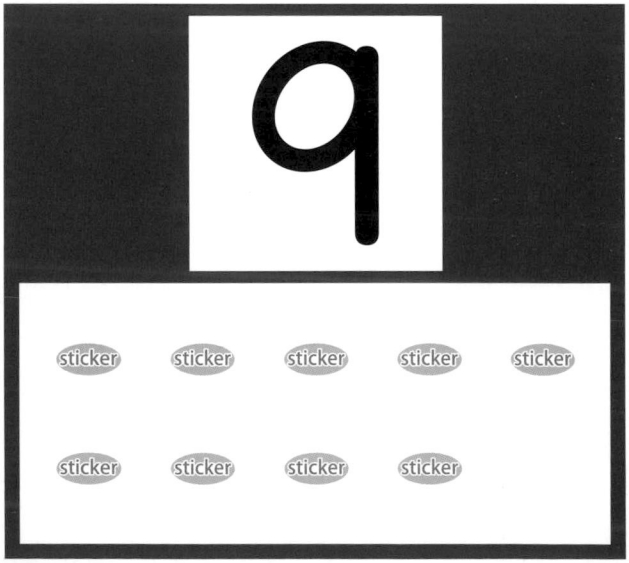

Numbers and Quantity

Add stickers on sticker so the number of flowers matches the number in the box.

10

sticker sticker sticker sticker sticker

sticker sticker sticker sticker sticker

Numbers

Count the Animals

Count the elephant and hippos in the picture and add the matching number stickers on sticker. Then, look at the number next to the lion. Add that many lion stickers to the picture.

sticker

sticker

sticker

Numbers

Count the Insects

Count the butterflies and ladybugs in the picture and add the matching number stickers on sticker. Then, look at the number next to the ant. Add that many ant stickers to the picture.

sticker sticker sticker sticker sticker sticker sticker sticker sticker sticker sticker

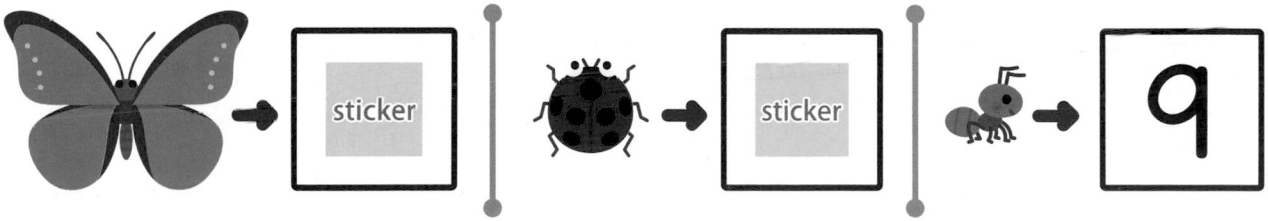

Number Match

Add stickers so there are four goldfish in each fishbowl.

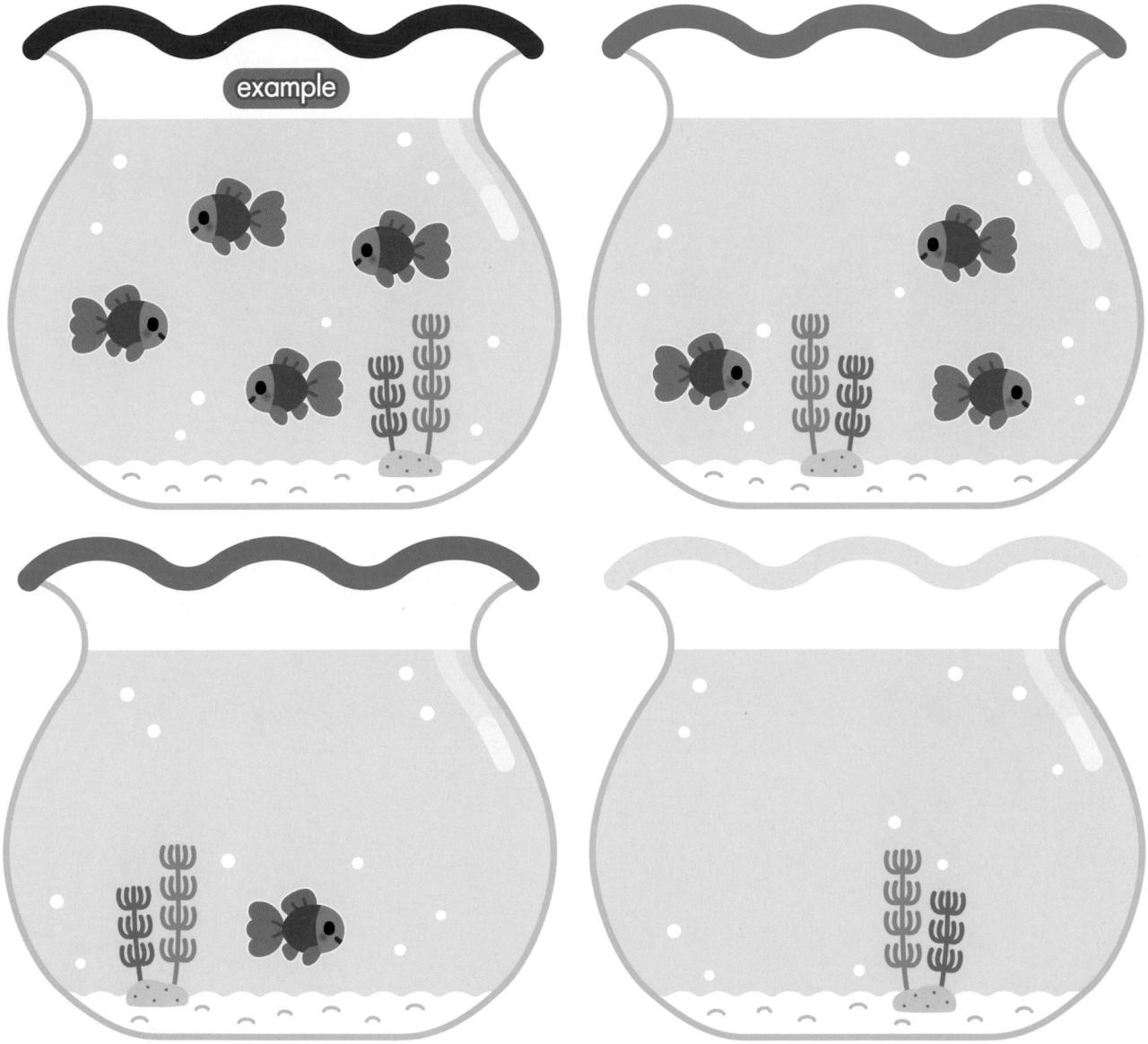

Maze Numbers

Squirrel's Favorite Food

Follow the path from ➡ to ➡. Always go in the direction of the larger number of treats. As you pass through each group, put a squirrel sticker on the space with the larger number. Then, put flower stickers wherever you'd like.

Maze Numbers

Number Maze

Follow the path from ➡ to ➡ in order of smallest to largest. As you go, put number stickers on the path. When finished, count the number of rabbits.

Snack Time

Feed each animal an apple, a banana, and a watermelon sticker.

Shapes in the Sea

Put the matching sticker on each shape to create sea creatures.

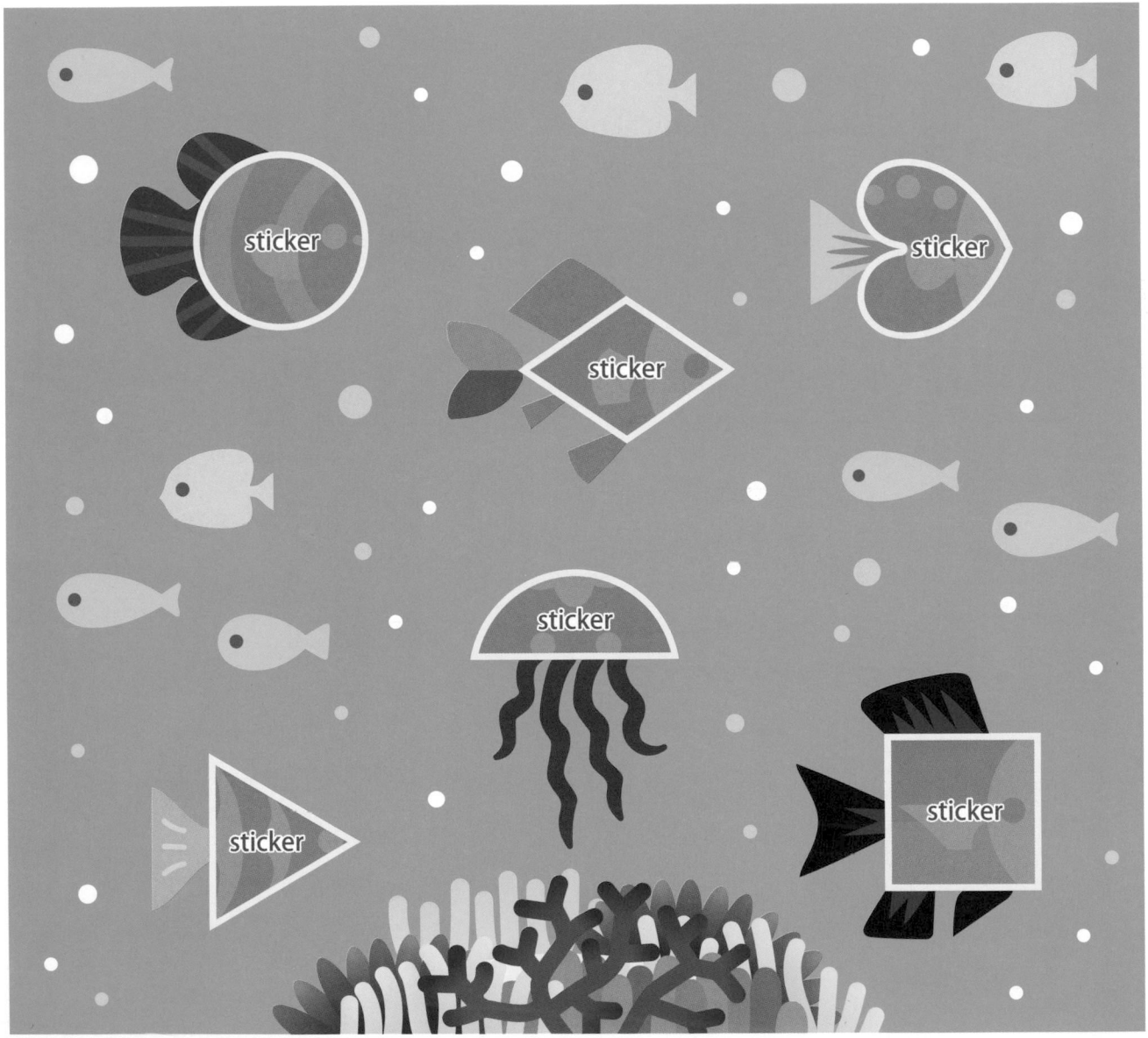

Shapes on the Farm

Put the matching sticker on each shape to create farm animals.

Maze

Fruit Maze

Follow the path from ➡ to ➡ while putting fruit stickers on their matching shadows.

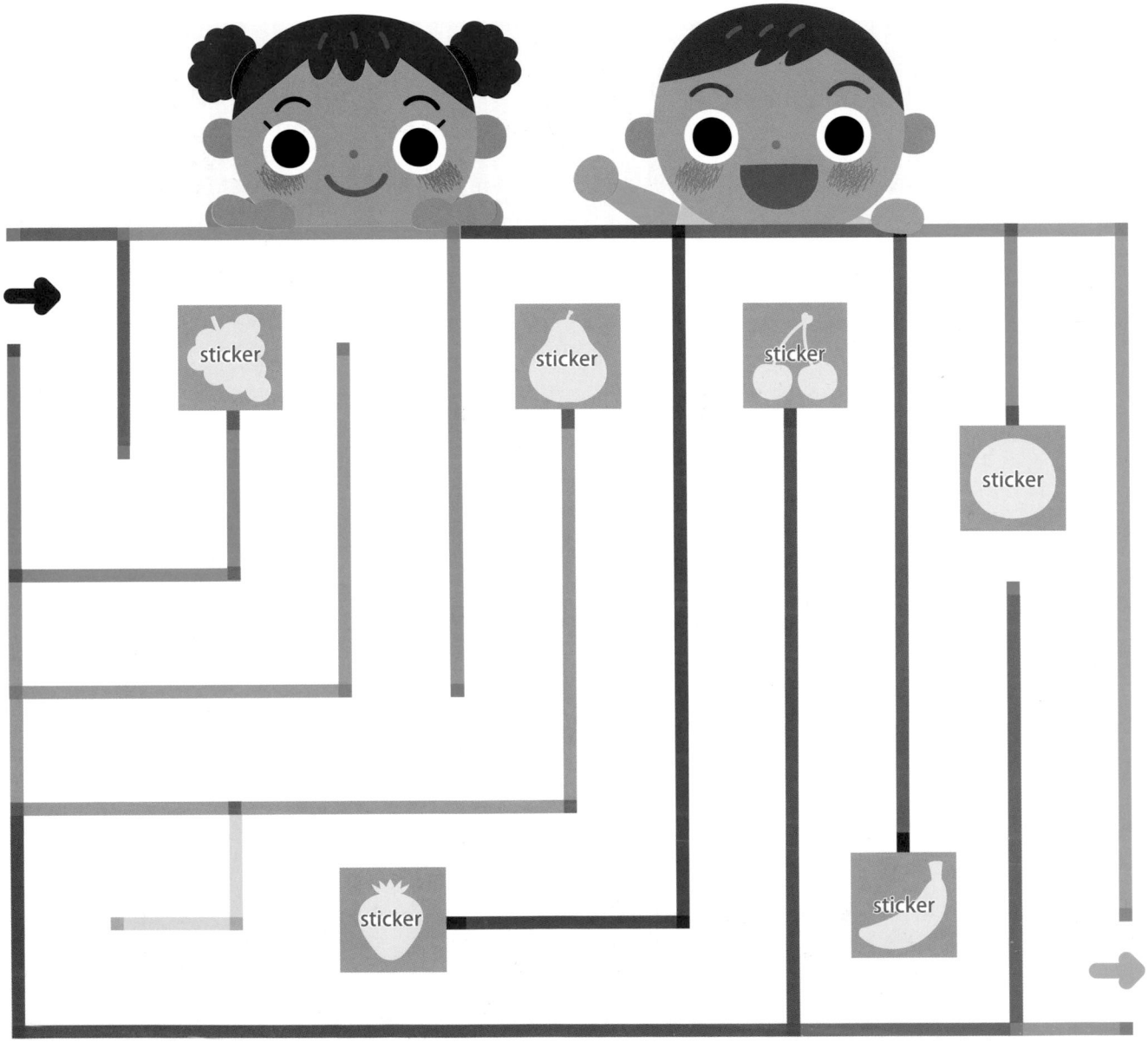

Maze

Choo Choo Train

Follow the path from ➡ to ➡ while putting stickers on the missing parts of the railroad track. Then, put animal stickers wherever you'd like.

sticker

sticker

sticker

sticker

sticker

Maze

Connect the Islands

Connect the islands with bridge stickers so the big mouse can get to the little mouse.

Maze

Haunted Maze

Follow the path from ➡ to ➡ while putting ladder stickers on the missing parts.

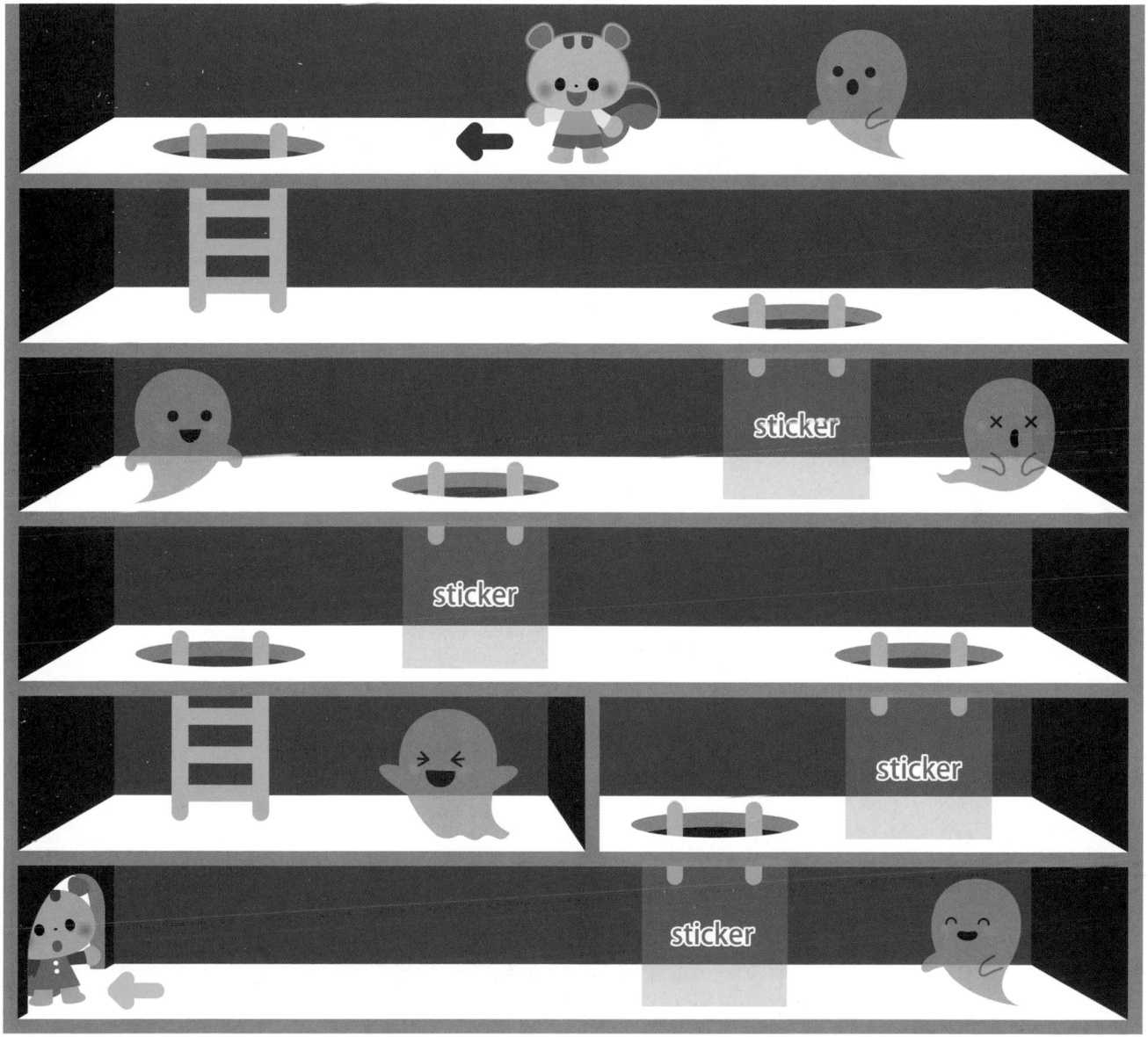

Matching Game

In the Garden

Put each insect sticker on its matching shadow.

Matching Game

In the Meadow

Put each animal sticker on its matching shadow. Then, put the extra stickers wherever you'd like.

Creativity

A Colorful Tree

Put leaf stickers on the tree. Then, add extra stickers to the scene.

Creativity

A Happy Hedgehog

Decorate the hedgehog's back with colorful △ stickers.

Shapes

Train Puzzle

Put stickers on the train so they match the shapes and colors.

sticker sticker sticker

sticker

sticker

sticker

sticker

sticker sticker

sticker

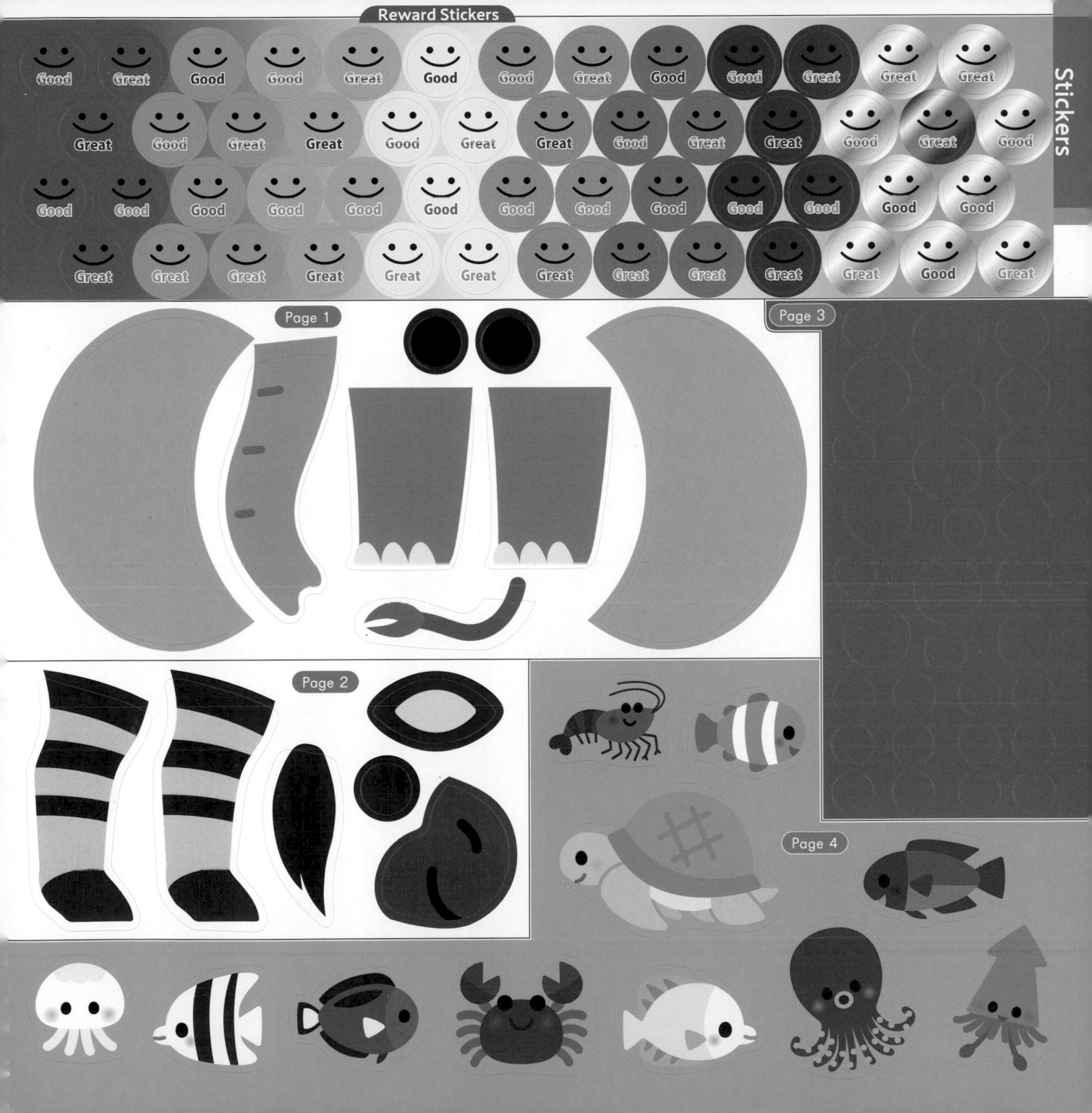
Reward Stickers
Stickers
Page 1
Page 2
Page 3
Page 4

Page 5

Page 6

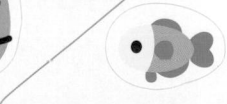

POLICE
TAXI
Page 9
Page 10
Page 12
Page 11
Page 13
Page 14
Page 16
Page 15
Page 17

Page 19
Page 20
Stickers
Page 18
Page 22
Page 21
Pago 23
Page 25
Page 24

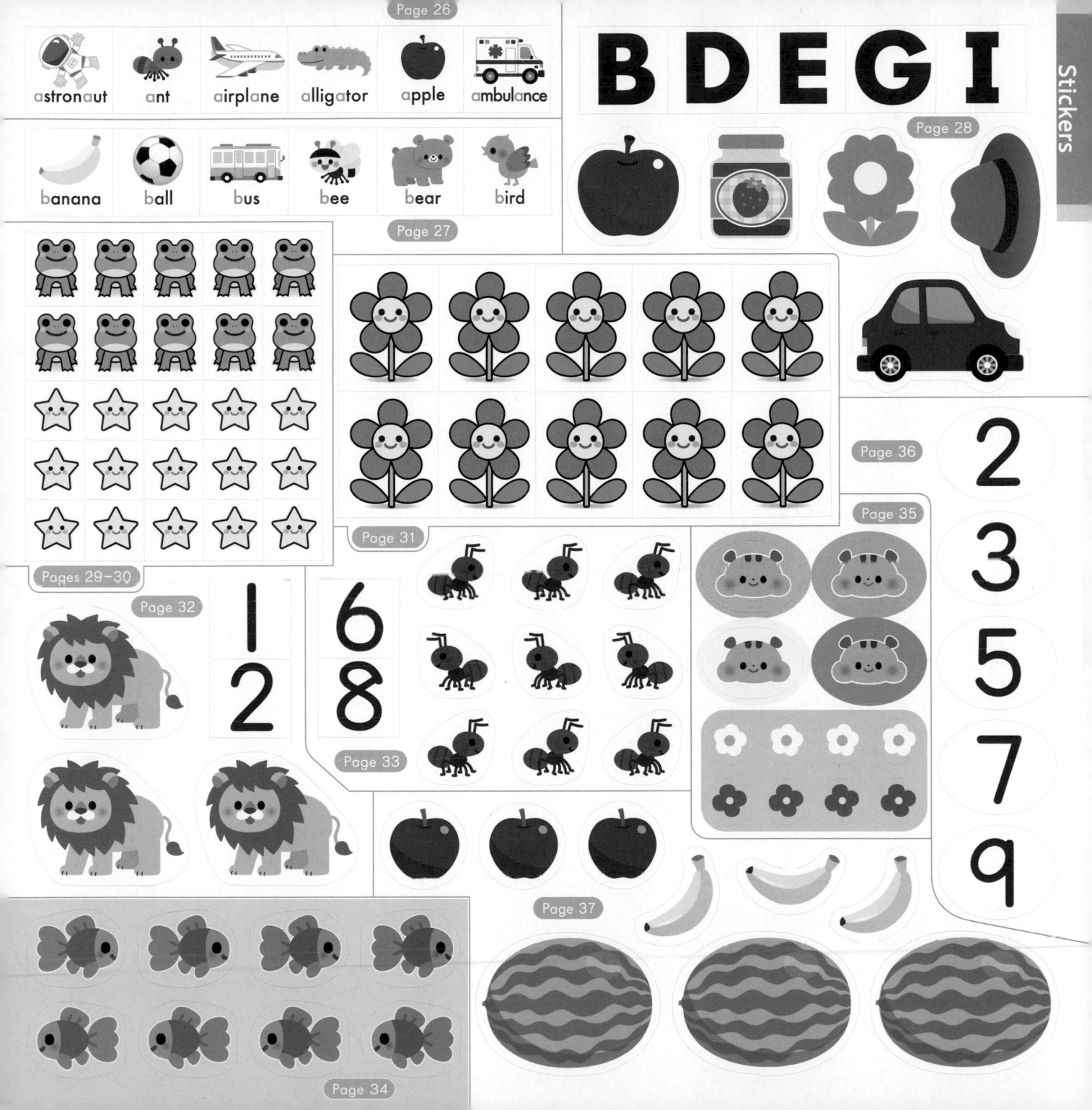
Page 26
astronaut
ant
airplane
alligator
apple
ambulance
banana
ball
bus
bee
bear
bird
Page 27
B D E G I
Page 28
Pages 29–30
Page 31
Page 32
1
2
6
8
Page 33
Page 34
Page 35
Page 36
2
3
5
7
9
Page 37

Stickers
Page 38
Page 39
Page 40
Page 41
Page 42
Page 43
Page 44

Page 45
Page 46
Page 47
Page 48